ICONS

BERLIN STYLE

BERLIN

Scenes   Interiors

STYLE
Details

PHOTOS **Eric Laignel**
PRODUCTION **Patricia Parinejad**
EDITOR **Angelika Taschen**

TASCHEN

KÖLN LONDON LOS ANGELES MADRID PARIS TOKYO

Front cover: No frills: in Erik Schmidt's dining room
Back cover: View to the west: on Paul Maenz's brekfast balcony

Couverture : Sans fiortures : la salle à manger d'Erik Schmidt
Dos de Couverture : Regard vers l'ouest : sur le balcon de Paul Maenz

Umschlagvorderseite: Schnörkellos: Im Esszimmer von Erik Schmidt
Umschlagrückseite: Blick nach Westen: Auf dem Frühstücksbalkon von Paul Maenz

Also available from TASCHEN:

Berlin Interiors
320 pages
3–8228–5885–7

To stay informed about upcoming TASCHEN titles, please request our magazine at
www.taschen.com or write to TASCHEN, Hohenzollernring 53, D–50672 Cologne,
Germany, Fax: +49-221-254919. We will be happy to send you a free copy of
our magazine which is filled with information about all of our books.

© 2004 TASCHEN GmbH
Hohenzollernring 53, D–50672 Köln
www.taschen.com

Concept and layout by Angelika Taschen, Cologne
Cover design by Angelika Taschen, Claudia Frey, Cologne
Generell project management by Stephanie Bischoff, Cologne
Texts by Christiane Reiter, Berlin
Lithography by Horst Neuzner, Cologne
English translation by Catherine Lara, Berlin
French translation by Thérèse Chatelain-Südkamp, Cologne

Printed in Italy
ISBN 3–8228–3227–8

CONTENTS SOMMAIRE INHALT

Can you fall in love with a city that receives you so indifferently and in an almost uncharming way? With endless streets through which the east wind is always blowing? And with an armada of construction cranes putting up terrible grey buildings? You can – but you need time. Berlin is no amour fou, no love at first sight. It doesn't reveal itself to the day-tripper who is spewed out of a tour bus in front of the Reichstag and hurries past all the monuments that are the backdrop for the evening news. It doesn't let people in on its secrets if they only follow the routes laid down in the travel guides. If you really want to have success with Berlin, you have to let yourself be carried along by the current of the city and learn to understand the brassy pragmatism of its inhabitants. You must stroll through dilapidated gates into blooming inner courtyards, open the art nouveau doors of hidden rear

TIME FOR BERLIN

Christiane Reiter

Peut-on tomber amoureux d'une ville qui vous accueille avec tant d'indifférence et, pourrait-on ajouter, d'une façon aussi peu charmante ? Avec ses avenues immenses où s'engouffre le vent d'est ? Et son armada de grues qui se dressent devant des bâtiments d'un gris terriblement morose. Il faut du temps pour découvrir la ville. Berlin n'est pas un coup de foudre. Il ne s'ouvre pas au visiteur d'un jour qui, éjecté de son car devant le Reichstag, se dépêche de voir tous ces fameux monuments qui, le soir aux informations, forment le décor devant lequel se tiennent les reporters. Il ne dévoile pas ses mystères à celui qui se contente de suivre les itinéraires indiqués dans les guides. Celui qui veut vraiment connaître Berlin doit musarder dans les rues et apprendre à connaître ses habitants pragmatiques et forts en gueule. Il doit passer sous les voûtes anciennes, se promener dans les cours fleuries, ouvrir les portes « Jugendstil » des petits

Kann man sich in eine Stadt verlieben, die einen so ungerührt und beinahe uncharmant empfängt? Mit endlosen Straßen, durch die ständig der Ostwind fegt? Und mit einer Armada von Baukränen vor schrecklich grauen Gebäuden? Man kann – aber man braucht Zeit. Berlin ist keine „amour fou", keine Liebe auf den ersten Blick. Es öffnet sich nicht dem Tagesbesucher, den ein Bus vor dem Reichstag ausspuckt und der an all den Monumenten vorbei hastet, die abends die Kulisse der Korrespondenten bilden. Es weiht niemanden in seine Geheimnisse ein, der nur den in Reiseführern eingezeichneten Routen folgt. Wer in Berlin wirklich ankommen möchte, muss sich durch die Stadt treiben lassen und den schnoddrigen Pragmatismus ihrer Bewohner verstehen lernen. Er muss durch verfallene Torbögen in blühende Innenhöfe spazieren, die Jugendstiltüren versteckter Gartenhäuser öffnen und in kleinen Parks im Schatten von

buildings, and sit in the shade of chestnut trees in little parks, until you can gradually put together the mosaic. Because every one of Berlin's neighbourhoods has a different world – nothing really matches, but everything somehow makes a whole. The flats of the city are as varied as its districts – Berlin doesn't stipulate any style and sets no limits. It offers an endless amount of space and makes everything possible: from Victorian salons to lofts, from ateliers to designer maisonettes. Since the passing of the exciting yet somewhat gruelling era of "boomtown Berlin", and the necessity for extravagance has receded back to normal metropolitan levels, you can once again, or for the first time, live here and nurture your personal style. And for many who had managed over time to fall a little bit in love with Berlin, then the city all of a sudden becomes much more: a love for life.

pavillons dissimulés dans les jardins et s'asseoir dans les parcs à l'ombre des châtaigniers pour que petit à petit il puisse réunir toutes les pierres de la mosaïque berlinoise. Car chaque quartier de Berlin constitue un univers différent, et si rien ne va ensemble tout finit par former quand même une unité. Les appartements de la ville sont tout aussi individuels que ses quartiers puisque Berlin n'impose aucune tendance stylistique ni ne fixe de limites. Tout semble donc possible : salons à l'ancienne, lofts, ateliers et duplex de designer. Depuis que la période excitante et quelque peu épuisante du boom de Berlin est révolue et que les extravagances ont été ramenées à un niveau normal pour une métropole, on peut de nouveau y vivre en toute tranquillité et y suivre son style personnel. Et pour tous ceux qui, au fil du temps, s'étaient déjà un peu épris de Berlin, la ville devient d'un seul coup bien davantage : un amour pour la vie.

Kastanien sitzen, bis er allmählich das Mosaik zusammensetzen kann. Denn mit jedem Kiez besitzt Berlin eine andere Welt – nichts passt wirklich zusammen, aber alles bildet irgendwie doch eine Einheit. So individuell wie ihre Viertel sind auch die Wohnungen der Stadt – Berlin schreibt keine Stilrichtung vor und setzt keine Grenzen. Es bietet unendlich viel Raum und macht alles möglich; vom Altbausalon bis zum Loft, vom Atelier bis zur Designermaisonette. Seit die aufregende und etwas aufreibende Ära der „Boomtown Berlin" vorbei ist und die Verpflichtung zur Extravaganz auf normales Metropolenmaß reguliert wurde, kann man hier auch wieder oder zum ersten Mal in aller Ruhe wohnen und seinen persönlichen Stil pflegen. Und für viele, die sich im Lauf der Zeit schon ein bisschen in Berlin verliebt hatten, wird die Stadt dann auf einmal noch viel mehr: eine Liebe fürs Leben.

"Morning on Alexanderplatz. The young hoods and streetwalkers. There's a lot of haggling; Threepenny Opera without songs."

Max Frisch in *Diary 1946-1949*

« Le matin sur l'Alexanderplatz. Les jeunes gangsters et les filles de joie. On par-lemente beaucoup ; un Opéra de quat'sous sans les chansons. »

Max Frisch dans *Journal intime 1946-1949*

„Vormittag am Alexanderplatz. Die jugendlichen Gangster und Dirnen. Es wird viel verhandelt; Dreigroschenoper ohne Songs."

Max Frisch in *Tagebuch 1946-1949*

HISTORIC SCENES

Scènes Historiques   Historische Szenen

10/11 Round and round: children in the Jüdenhof, around 1930. *Toujours en rond : des enfants dans la Jüdenhof, la Cour des juifs, vers 1930.* Immer im Kreis: Kinder auf dem Jüdenhof, um 1930.

12/13 Pack the bathing costumes: two women by the lake, 1920. *Emporte tes affaires de bain : deux dames près du lac, 1920.* Pack die Badekleider ein: Zwei Damen am See, 1920.

14/15 Prime location: sunbathing on a rooftop lawn, 1926. *Un endroit idéal : bain de soleil sur un toit, 1926.* In bester Lage: Sonnenbad auf einer Dachwiese, 1926.

16/17 The art of merry-making: in Herwarth Walden's gallery "Der Sturm", 1923. *L'art de la fête : dans la galerie « Der Sturm » de Herwarth Walden, 1923.* Die Kunst des Feierns: In Herwarth Waldens Galerie „Der Sturm", 1923.

18/19 Jubilation a long time gone: BDM girls waiting for Hitler, 1938. *Des cris de joie qui se sont tus depuis longtemps : jeunes filles BDM attendant Hitler, 1938.* Jubel, längst vergangen: BDM-Mädchen warten auf Hitler, 1938.

20/21 Dancing on the rubble: The music plays again, 1945. *Danse sur des ruines : on rejoue de la musique, 1945.* Tanz auf den Trümmern: Die Musik spielt wieder, 1945.

22/23 We are Berliners: Kennedy, Brandt and Adenauer, 1963. *Nous sommes des Berlinois : Kennedy, Brandt et Adenauer, 1963.* Wir sind Berliner: Kennedy, Brandt und Adenauer, 1963.

24/25 New perspectives: demolition of the Wall at the Brandenburg Gate, 1990. *Nouvelles perspectives : démolition du Mur à la Porte de Brandebourg, 1990.* Neue Perspektiven: Abriss der Mauer am Brandenburger Tor, 1990.

26/27 In the brilliance of the night: the Philharmonie and Potsdamer Platz, 2000. *Dans l'éclat de la nuit : la philharmonie et le Potsdamer Platz, 2000.* Im Glanz der Nacht: Philharmonie und Potsdamer Platz, 2000.

28/29 View to the west: on Paul Maenz's breakfast balcony. *Regard vers l'ouest : sur le balcon de Paul Maenz.* Blick nach Westen: Auf dem Frühstücksbalkon von Paul Maenz.

30 Our doors are always open: entrance to the art nouveau hotel, "Askanischer Hof". *Des portes toujours ouvertes : entrée de l'hôtel art nouveau « Askanischer Hof ».* Stets offene Türen: Eingang zum Jugendstilhotel „Askanischer Hof".

"Somewhere a room, all in white. Is it a room… or a flower garden? Full of lilac, azaleas, tulips, snowdrops – and all sorts."

Alfred Kerr in *From the Diary of a Berliner*

« Quelque part une pièce, toute blanche. Est-ce bien une pièce... ou un jardin fleuri ? Plein de lilas, d'azalées, de tulipes, de perce-neige – et de toutes sortes de choses. »

Alfred Kerr dans *Du journal intime d'un Berlinois*

„Irgendwo ein Zimmer, ganz in Weiß. Ist es ein Zimmer... oder ein Blumengarten? Voll von Flieder, Azaleen, Tulpen, Schneeglöckchen – und allerhand."

Alfred Kerr in *Aus dem Tagebuch eines Berliners*

BERLIN INTERIORS

Intérieurs à Berlin Berliner Interieurs

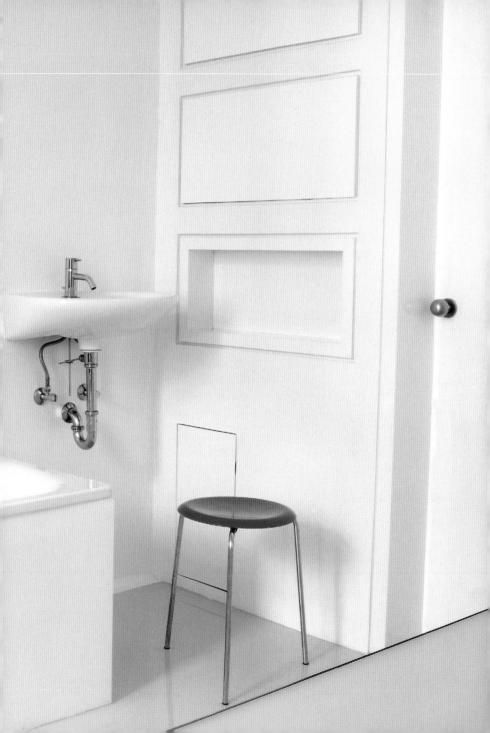

Just Married

34/35 Shining example: the mirrored hall at the Russian Embassy. *Brille de tous ses feux : la salle des miroirs de l'ambassade de Russie.* Leuchtendes Beispiel: Der Spiegelsaal der Russischen Botschaft.

36/37 Sparkling: in the silver-coloured vestibule of the Russian Embassy. *Étincelant : le vestibule argenté de l'ambassade de Russie.* Funkelnd: Im silberfarbenen Vestibül der Russischen Botschaft.

38/39 On the way up: the sumptuous stairwell of the Russian Embassy. *Vers les étages supérieurs : la somptueuse cage d'escalier de l'ambassade de Russie.* Auf dem Weg nach oben: Das glamouröse Treppenhaus der Russischen Botschaft.

40/41 Pages and pages of memories: in Nicolaus Sombart's salon. *Que de souvenirs : dans le salon de Nicolaus Sombart.* Seitenweise Erinnerungen: Im Salon von Nicolaus Sombart.

42/43 In bloom: view of a planted roof in front of Max Raabe's loft. *Que de verdure : vue sur un toit devant le loft de Max Raabe.* Blütezeit: Blick auf ein begrüntes Dach vor Max Raabes Loft.

44/45 Culture up to the ceiling: in Max Raabe's reading and music room. *De la culture jusqu'au plafond : dans le salon de lecture et de musique de Max Raabe.* Kultur bis unter die Decke: Im Lese- und Musikzimmer von Max Raabe.

46/47 Favourite spot: at Max Raabe's black-framed fireplace. *L'endroit préféré : près de la cheminée au cadre noir de Max Raabe.* Lieblingsplatz: An Max Raabes schwarz gerahmten Kamin.

48/49 Workplace: The pieces for the Palast Orchester are composed on the grand piano. *Le lieu de travail : c'est sur ce piano que sont composés les morceaux pour le Palast Orchester.* Arbeitsplatz: Am Flügel entstehen die Stücke für das Palast Orchester.

50/51 Berlin backdrop: Artists are guests at the "Askanischer Hof". *Coulisses berlinoises : le « Askanischer Hof » est le rendez-vous des artistes.* Berliner Kulisse: Im "Askanischen Hof" sind Künstler zu Gast.

52/53 A gem: the tiled store of the architect Andreas Hierholzer. *Un petit bijou : le poêle de faïence de l'architecte Andreas Hierholzer.* Schmuckstück: Der Kachelofen des Architekten Andreas Hierholzer.

54/55 Beneath a coloured stucco ceiling: pictures in Andreas Hierholzer's flat. *Sous des moulures colorées : tableaux dans l'appartement d'Andreas Hierholzer.* Unter farbigem Stuck: Bilder in der Wohnung von Andreas Hierholzer.

56/57 Framework: Olaf Lemke is a dealer in antique frames. *Il sait encadrer : Olaf Lemke est marchand de cadres anciens.* Mit Fassung getragen: Olaf Lemke ist Händler für antike Rahmen.

58/59 A suitable setting: In the "Berlin room" Olaf Lemke advises his customers. *Choisir le cadre idéal : au « Berliner Zimmer » Olaf Lemke conseille ses clients.* Passender Rahmen: Im „Berliner Zimmer" berät Olaf Lemke seine Kunden.

60/61 Photo gallery: in the bedroom of Anne Maria Jagdfeld. *Galerie de photos : dans la chambre d'Anne Maria Jagdfeld.* Fotogalerie: Im Schlafzimmer von Anne Maria Jagdfeld.

62/63 Own creations: Anne Maria Jagdfeld designed the wardrobes herself. *Créations personnelles : Anne Maria Jagdfeld a dessiné elle-même les armoires.* Eigenkreationen: Die Schränke hat Anne Maria Jagdfeld selbst entworfen.

64/65 Bathed in golden light: the dining room of Anne Maria Jagdfeld. *Plongée dans une lumière dorée : la salle à manger d'Anne Maria Jagdfeld.* In goldenes Licht getaucht: Das Esszimmer von Anne Maria Jagdfeld.

66/67 At home in nature: Star florist Frank Stüve lives here. *Une maison dans la verdure : celle de Frank Stüve, star des fleuristes.* Ein Zuhause im Grünen: Hier lebt der Starflorist Frank Stüve.

68/69 Absolute clarity: Simple forms and unexpected themes dominate here. *Aucune méprise possible : ici ce sont les formes simples et les motifs inattendus qui dominent.* Deutlich: Hier dominieren schlichte Formen und unerwartete Motive.

70/71 Loge seat: Paul Maenz's balcony overlooks the Brandenburg Gate. *Une bonne place : le balcon de Paul Maenz donne directement sur la Porte de Brandebourg.* Logenplatz: Der Balkon von Paul Maenz liegt direkt am Brandenburger Tor.

72/73 Wide-eyed: *"Jeune femme étonnée"* in Paul Maenz's flat. *De grands yeux : « Jeune femme étonnée » dans l'appartement de Paul Maenz.* Mit großen Augen: „Jeune femme étonnée" in der Wohnung von Paul Maenz.

74/75 Glass times: in the dining room of gallery owner Max Hetzler. *Toute de verre : la salle à manger du galeriste Max Hetzler.* Gläserne Zeiten: Im Esszimmer des Galeristen Max Hetzler.

76/77 A modern classic: Max Hetzler is interested in clear lines and broad expanses. *Un classique moderne : Max Hetzler a choisi les lignes claires et les grands espaces.* Moderne Klassiker: Max Hetzler setzt auf klare Linien und große Flächen.

78/79 A dash of colour: in Max Hetzler's bedroom, furniture by Jean Prouvé. *Touches de couleur : les meubles de Jean Prouvé dans la chambre de Max Hetzler.* Farbtupfer: Im Schlafzimmer von Max Hetzler stehen Möbel von Jean Prouvé.

80/81 Welcome to the labyrinth: at the house of designer Heike Mühlhaus and Dr. Motte. *Bienvenue dans le labyrinthe : chez la créatrice Heike Mühlhaus et le dr Motte.* Willkommen im Labyrinth: Bei der Designerin Heike Mühlhaus und dr Motte.

82/83 Think pink: Designer Heike Mühlhaus and Dr. Motte had an outer wall painted pink. *Think pink : la créatrice Heike Mühlhaus et le dr Motte ont fait repeindre en rose un mur de la façade.* Think pink: Eine Außenwand ließen die Designerin Heike Mühlhaus und Dr. Motte rosa streichen.

84/85 In the picture: works by Sean Landers and Tal R. in Stephan Landwehr's loft. *Bien présentés : les travaux de Sean Landers et de Tal R. dans le loft de Stephan Landwehr.* Gut im Bild: Werke von Sean Landers und Tal R. im Loft von Stephan Landwehr.

86/87 The dreams of the clown: in Stephan Landwehr's sleeping space. *Les songes du clown : dans la chambre de Stephan Landwehr.* Die Träume des Clowns: Im Schlafraum von Stephan Landwehr.

88/89 Berlin's southern side: Gisela von Schenk's terrace. *Le Sud à Berlin : la terrasse de Gisela von Schenk.* Die Terrasse von Gisela von Schenk.

90/91 In the white house: Gisela von Schenk combines various styles. *Dans la maison blanche : Gisela von Schenk marie différents styles.* Im weißen Haus: Gisela von Schenk verbindet unterschiedliche Stile.

92/93 Construction-site kitchen: Sabina Nordalm designed the pink kitchen units herself. *La cuisine : Sabina Nordalm a conçu elle-même les encastrements en rose.* Baustelle Küche: Die Zeile in Rosé hat Sabina Nordalm selbst gestaltet.

94/95 Blue hour: Even the CD case comes from Nordalm's firm, "raumwerk". *In the blues : l'étagère pour les disques compact provient elle aussi de la firme de Nordalm « raumwerk ».* Blaue Pause: Auch das CD-Regal stammt aus Nordalms Firma „raumwerk".

96/97 Purist: In this bathroom the walls were lacquered in white, not tiled. *Puriste : dans cette salle de bains, les murs n'ont pas été carrelés mais laqués de blanc.* Puristisch: In diesem Bad wurden die Wände weiß lackiert, nicht gefliest.

98/99 Space and distance: Dark walls were replaced by supporting columns. *Espace et profondeur : les murs sombres ont été remplacés par des piliers porteurs.* Raum und Weite: Dunkle Mauern wurden durch tragende Stützen ersetzt.

100/101 Fascination with the East: Erik Schmidt lives in a typical concrete slab building built in 1968. *La nostalgie de la RDA : Erik Schmidt vit dans un grand ensemble datant de 1968.* Faszination Osten: Erik Schmidt lebt in einem Plattenbau anno 1968.

102/103 Wall variations: Erik Schmidt looks at bare concrete and old wallpaper designs. *Variations murales : Erik Schmidt a vue sur du béton et de vieux motifs de papiers peints.* Wand-Variationen: Erik Schmidt blickt auf bloßen Beton und alte Tapetenmuster.

104/105 "Eddie" keeps watch over the bubble chairs in designer Stefan Fuhrmann's flat. *Le gardien : « Eddie » veille sur le fauteuil bubble dans l'appartement du designer Stefan Fuhrmann.* „Eddie" bewacht die Bubble-Sessel in der Wohnung von Designer Stefan Fuhrmann.

106/107 Three in one: This table by Ralf Schmerberg is for eating, working and celebrating. *Trois en une : cette table de Ralf Schmerberg sert à manger, à travailler et à faire la fête.* Drei in einem: An diesem Tisch von Ralf Schmerberg wird gegessen, gearbeitet und gefeiert.

108/109 Inspiration: In the "poetry room", poems hang like washing put out to dry. *Inspiration : dans la « salle de la poésie », les poèmes sont suspendus comme du linge à sécher.* Inspiration: Im „Poem-Raum" hängen Gedichte wie Wäsche an der Leine.

110/111 Coloured felt: This is how the sun rises in Christine Birkle's kitchen. *Feutre de couleur : soleil levant dans la cuisine de Christine Birkle.* Farbiger Filz: So geht in der Küche von Christine Birkle die Sonne auf.

112/113 Mixed materials: Felt and wood turn the living room into a source of warmth. *Mélange de matériaux : feutre et bois font de la salle de séjour une source de chaleur.* Materialmix: Filz und Holz machen das Wohnzimmer zur Wärmequelle.

114/115 The gleam of gold: Accessories from the flea market provide the salon with its finishing touches. *L'éclat de l'or : les accessoires du marché aux puces confèrent au salon tout son caractère.* Der Glanz des Goldes: Accessoires vom Trödel verleihen dem Salon Schliff.

116/117 Kindled: Elegant dinners held by Udo Walz at his fireplace remain unforgettable. *Brillant de tous leurs feux: chez Udo Walz les dîners élégants .* Entflammt: Elegante Dinner bei Udo Walz.

118/119 Kitsch is art: in Laura Kikauka's "love grotto". *Kitsch égale art: la « grotte d'amour » de Laura Kikauka.* Kitsch ist Kunst: In der „Liebesgrotte" von Laura Kikauka.

120/121 A gift from father: Edith Lohse's dining room furniture was a wedding present. *Un cadeau du père : Edith Lohse reçut ses meubles de salle à manger pour son mariage .* Ein Geschenk des Vaters: Die Esszimmermöbel bekam Edith Lohse zur Hochzeit.

122/123 Painting and music: two passions of the artist Jonathan Meese. *La peinture et la musique : deux passions de l'artiste Jonathan Meese.* Malen und Musik: Zwei Leidenschaften des Künstlers Jonathan Meese.

124/125 Bedside Art: in the bedroom of Michel Würthle, owner of the "Paris Bar". *De l'art près du lit : dans la chambre de Michel Würthle, patron du « Paris Bar ».* Kunst am Bett: Im Schlafzimmer von Michel Würthle, Wirt der „Paris Bar".

126/127 Freedom in the open: alternative living in Kreuzberg. *Liberté en plein air : autre façon de vivre à Kreuzberg.* Freiheit im Freien: Alternatives Wohnen mitten in Kreuzberg.

128/129 Little kingdom: in the allotment colony, "Am Volkspark Prenzlauer Berg". *Un petit royaume bien à soi : les jardins ouvriers « Am Volkspark Prenzlauer Berg ».* Kleines Reich: In der Schrebergartensiedlung „Am Volkspark Prenzlauer Berg".

130/131 Cooking niche: The foliage, including kitchen, measures 30 square metres. *Coin cuisine : la maisonnette fait 30 mètres carrés – cuisine comprise.* Kochnische: 30 Quadratmeter misst die Laube – inklusive Küche.

132/133 Hiding place: Hans Rosenthal lived here for two years during the Nazi period. *Cachette : c'est ici que vécut Hans Rosenthal pendant deux ans sous les nazis.* Versteck: Hier lebte Hans Rosenthal zwei Jahre während der Nazizeit.

134/135 Living on the water: Michael Haberkorn lives on a houseboat. *Habiter sur l'eau : Michael Haberkorn vit dans un houseboat.* Wohnen auf dem Wasser: Michael Haberkorn lebt auf einem Hausboot.

136/137 Quiet tones: Haberkorn even invites guests on board for music evenings. *Soirée musicale : à bord, Haberkorn invite à faire de la musique.* Leise Töne: An Bord lädt Haberkorn sogar zu Hausmusikabenden ein.

138/139 Idyll on the lake: Dieter Mann's boathouse is as pretty as a picture. *Idylle sur le lac : le house-boat de Dieter Mann est de toute beauté.* Idylle am See: Dieter Manns Boots-haus ist so schön wie gemalt.

140/141 The way of the seaman: wood planks and lifebelts inside the boathouse. *Il était un petit navire: bordages en bois et bouée de sauvetage à l'intérieur du house-boat.* Nach Seemannsart: Holzplanken und Rettungsring im Inneren des Bootshauses.

142/143 Country-house style: The interior comes from the Potsdam shop, "Garten-träume". *Style campagnard : l'intérieur provient du magasin de Potsdam « Gartenträume ».* Landhausstil: Das Interieur stammt aus dem Potsdamer Geschäft „Gartenträume".

144/145 Perfect panorama: The lake begins right in front of the terrace. *Un panorama par-fait : le lac se trouve juste devant la terrasse.* Perfektes Panorama: Gleich vor der Terrasse beginnt der See.

146/147 Dream house: The architect Werner Aisslinger lives in a 1916 villa. *Maison de rêve: l'architecte Werner Aisslinger vit dans une villa datant de 1916.* Traumhaus: Der Architekt Werner Aisslinger lebt in einer Villa anno 1916.

148/149 Success story: Aisslinger's "Juli" chairs in his own dining room. *L'histoire d'une réussite : les chaises « Juli » d'Aisslinger dans sa salle à manger.* Erfolgsgeschichte: Aisslingers Stühle „Juli" in seinem eigenen Esszimmer.

150/151 Hunting trophy: a fox fur for bedspread in Aisslinger's bedroom. *Trophée de chasse : une couverture en renard dans la chambre d'Aisslinger.* Jagdtrophäe: Eine Decke aus Fuchsfell in Aisslingers Schlafzimmer.

152/153 Late season: An autumn mood reigns in the garden. *L'arrière-saison : ambiance automnale dans le jardin.* Nach-saison: Im Garten herrscht Herbststimmung.

"In a corner between the shelves, directly behind a revolving bookstand, the corner of a shining red dress was showing."

Vladimir Nabokov in *Laughter in the Dark*

« *Dans un coin entre les étagères, juste derrière un porte-livres pivotant, dépassait le bout d'une robe d'un rouge éclatant.* »

Vladimir Nabokov dans *Chambre obscure*

„*In einer Ecke zwischen den Regalen, direkt hinter einem drehbaren Bücherständer, schaute der Zipfel eines leuchtendroten Kleides hervor.*"

Vladimir Nabokov in *Gelächter im Dunkel*

CHARMING DETAILS

Détails charmants　Charmante Details

**Rechts
vor links**

ICH HABE EINEN TRAUM

28

11. Haakel | Müller | Silberfer | Ezenhöfer/Bur.
10. Nähel | Lehner | Knebel | Rothe
9. Klement | Ringmann | Bachobletsch/Knath | Liepe
8. Jacobi | Heimbold | Forster | Bel
7. Priess | Graf | Kahler | Freitag
6. Linzbach | Rigo | Schleimer | Klaus
5. Kletz | Heydecke | Faugstadt | Schuldenbach
4. Keiting | Peter | Kapahnke | Marschnak
3. Haase & Kühnelt | Albuchewski | Hoffmann | Gössl/Lange
2. Hänschke/Kuhn | Hütjerobalski | Büttcher | Westrow
1. Kranzik | Schuldner | BRENDEL | Schmidt

WBF

28

Platz der Vereinten Nationen

162 Luminosity: lampshades on five feet. *Intensité lumineuse : abat-jour sur cinq pieds.* Leuchtkraft: Lampenschirm auf fünf Füßen.

163 Directly in view: black-and-white portrait and Ibo statue. *Accrochent l'œil : portrait en noir et blanc et statue Ibo.* Fest im Blick: Schwarz-Weiß-Portrait und Ibo-Statue.

164 Handwritten: a dilapidated Berlin stairwell. *Avec dédicaces : cage d'escalier berlinoise assez délabrée.* Mit Handschrift: Verfallenes Berliner Treppenhaus.

166 Ready to talk: an antique telephone at Andreas Hierholzer's. *Prêt pour la conversation : téléphone ancien chez Andreas Hierholzer.* Gesprächsbereit: Antikes Telefon bei Andreas Hierholzer.

167 Time's witnesses: newspaper pages from the year 1895 on Hierholzer's walls. *Témoins de leur temps : pages de journal datant de 1895 sur les murs de Hierholzer.* Zeitzeugen: Zeitungsseiten aus dem Jahr 1895 an Hierholzers Wänden.

168 Silent guards: fuses and the electricity meter at Edith Lohse's. *Gardiens muets : fusibles et compteur électrique chez Edith Lohse.* Stumme Wächter: Sicherungen und Stromzähler bei Edith Lohse.

170 Richly decorated: Andreas Hierholzer's tiled stove. *Richement décoré : poêle de faïence d'Andreas Hierholzer.* Reich verziert: Der Kachelofen von Andreas Hierholzer.

171 Dine more beautifully: shining gold art over the table. *Pour le plaisir des yeux : œuvres d'art étincelantes au-dessus de la table.* Schöner essen: Goldglänzende Kunst über dem Tisch.

172 Stuff of dreams: an old newspaper clipping. *Pour rêver : un vieil article de journal.* Zum Träumen: Alter Zeitungsausschnitt.

174 Black disc: music from times past. *Sur microsillon : une musique du temps passé.* Schwarze Scheibe: Musik aus vergangenen Zeiten.

175 Gallery of ancestors: the family photos of Edith Lohse. *Galerie des ancêtres : photos de famille d'Edith Lohse.* Ahnengalerie: Familienfotos von Edith Lohse.

176 Lamp and radio: in the hotel "Askanischer Hof". *Lampe et radio : à l'hôtel « Askanischer Hof ».* Lampe und Radio: Im Hotel „Askanischer Hof".

178 Chequered: clock in Erik Schmidt's flat. *A carreaux : pendule dans l'appartement d'Erik Schmidt.* Kariert: Uhr in der Wohnung von Erik Schmidt.

179 Unified design: nameplate on a Communist-era concrete slab building. *Design uniforme : sonnette dans un grand ensemble.* Einheitsdesign: Klingelschild am Plattenbau.

180 No frills: in Erik Schmidt's dining room. *Sans fioritures : la salle à manger d'Erik Schmidt.* Schnörkellos: Im Esszimmer von Erik Schmidt.

182 Sextet: wall decoration at Gisela von Schenk's. *Sextuor : décoration murale chez Gisela von Schenk.* Sextett: Wandschmuck bei Gisela von Schenk.

183 Green accent: next to Gisela von Schenk's sofa. *Accent de vert : à côté du canapé de Gisela von Schenk.* Akzent in Grün: Neben dem Sofa von Gisela von Schenk.

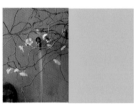

184 Artificial flowers: a southern-style bathroom. *Fleurs artificielle : salle de bains d'inspiration méridionale.* Künstliche Blüten: Südlich angehauchtes Badezimmer.

186 Folding chairs: in front of a garden-house on Prenzlauer Berg. *Chaises pliantes : devant une maisonnette de jardin à Prenzlauer Berg.* Klappstühle: Vor einer Laube am Prenzlauer Berg.

187 Clear announcement: washbasin in the allotment colony. *Invitation à la propreté : lavabo dans le jardin ouvrier.* Klare Ansage: Waschbecken im Schrebergarten.

188 Picture-perfect background: toilet throne in the community garden. *Papier peint à motif photographique : le trône des toilettes dans les jardins ouvriers.* Fototapete im Rücken: Toiletten-Thron in den Schrebergärten.

Berlin Interiors
Ed. Angelika Taschen / Ingeborg
Wiensowski / Hardcover, 320 pp. /
€ 29.99 / $ 39.99 / £ 24.99 /
¥ 5.900

London Interiors
Ed. Angelika Taschen / Jane
Edwards / Hardcover, 304 pp. /
€ 29.99 / $ 39.99 / £ 24.99 /
¥ 5.900

Miami Interiors
Ed. Angelika Taschen / Patricia
Parinejad / Hardcover, 320 pp. /
€ 29.99 / $ 39.99 / £ 24.99 /
¥ 5.900

"...an elegant and enlightening addition
for any coffee table."
—*Homes & Living*, Perth, on *Berlin Interiors*

"Buy them all and add some pleasure to your life."

All-American Ads 40s
Ed. Jim Heimann

All-American Ads 50s
Ed. Jim Heimann

All-American Ads 60s
Ed. Jim Heimann

Angels
Gilles Néret

Architecture Now!
Ed. Philip Jodidio

Art Now
Eds. Burkhard Riemschneider,
Uta Grosenick

Berlin Style
Ed. Angelika Taschen

Chairs
Charlotte & Peter Fiell

Design of the 20th Century
Charlotte & Peter Fiell

Design for the 21st Century
Charlotte & Peter Fiell

Devils
Gilles Néret

Digital Beauties
Ed. Julius Wiedemann

Robert Doisneau
Ed. Jean-Claude Gautrand

East German Design
Ralf Ulrich / Photos: Ernst
Hedler

Eccentric Style
Ed. Angelika Taschen

Fashion
Ed. The Kyoto Costume
Institute

HR Giger
HR Giger

Graphic Design
Ed. Charlotte & Peter Fiell

Grand Tour
Harry Seidler,
Ed. Peter Gössel

Havana Style
Ed. Angelika Taschen

Homo Art
Gilles Néret

Hot Rods
Ed. Coco Shinomiya

Hula
Ed. Jim Heimann

India Bazaar
Samantha Harrison,
Bari Kumar

Industrial Design
Charlotte & Peter Fiell

Japanese Beauties
Ed. Alex Gross

Kitchen Kitsch
Ed. Jim Heimann

Krazy Kids' Food
Eds. Steve Roden,
Dan Goodsell

Las Vegas
Ed. Jim Heimann

Mexicana
Ed. Jim Heimann

Morocco Style
Ed. Angelika Taschen

**Extra/Ordinary Objects,
Vol. I**
Ed. Colors Magazine

**Extra/Ordinary Objects,
Vol. II**
Ed. Colors Magazine

Paris Style
Ed. Angelika Taschen

Penguin
Frans Lanting

Photo Icons, Vol. I
Hans-Michael Koetzle

Photo Icons, Vol. II
Hans-Michael Koetzle

20th Century Photography
Museum Ludwig Cologne

Pin-Ups
Ed. Burkhard Riemschneider

Provence Style
Ed. Angelika Taschen

Pussycats
Gilles Néret

Safari Style
Ed. Angelika Taschen

Seaside Style
Ed. Angelika Taschen

Albertus Seba. Butterflies
Irmgard Müsch

**Albertus Seba. Shells &
Corals**
Irmgard Müsch

Starck
Ed Mae Cooper, Pierre Doze,
Elisabeth Laville

Surfing
Ed. Jim Heimann

Sydney Style
Ed. Angelika Taschen

Tattoos
Ed. Henk Schiffmacher

Tiffany
Jacob Baal-Teshuva

Tiki Style
Sven Kirsten

Tuscany Style
Ed. Angelika Taschen

Women Artists
in the 20th and 21st Century
Ed. Uta Grosenick

★

ICONS